Emma

JANE AUSTEN

Level 4

Retold by Annette Barnes
Series Editors: Andy Hopkins and Jocelyn Potter

Pearson Education Limited
Edinburgh Gate, Harlow,
Essex CM20 2JE, England
and Associated Companies throughout the world.

ISBN: 978-1-4058-8214-9

First published 1816
This adaptation first published by Penguin Books 1998
Published by Addison Wesley Longman Limited and Penguin Books Ltd 1998
New edition first published 1999
This edition first published 2008

3 5 7 9 10 8 6 4 2

Typeset by Graphicraft Ltd, Hong Kong
Set in 11/14pt Bembo
Printed in China
SWTC/02

Published by Pearson Education Ltd in association with
Penguin Books Ltd, both companies being subsidiaries of Pearson Plc

For a complete list of the titles available in the Penguin Readers series please write to your local
Pearson Longman office or to: Penguin Readers Marketing Department, Pearson Education,
Edinburgh Gate, Harlow, Essex CM20 2JE, England.

Contents

Introduction

'Harriet Smith has no family and no money. Robert Martin was a good match for her, Emma. Until she met you, she thought of nothing better for herself, but you have filled her head with ideas of high society and of how beautiful she is.'

Emma Woodhouse is twenty-one years old, beautiful, clever and rich. She amuses herself by trying to arrange marriages between her friends and neighbours.

When Emma meets the seventeen-year-old Harriet Smith, she can see that Harriet needs her help finding a partner. Poor Harriet has no living family and no money. But Emma thinks that Harriet deserves a better man than Robert Martin, a farmer. Robert asks Harriet to marry him after Emma's friend, Mr Knightley, advises him to do so. Mr Knightley is not pleased when he learns that Emma has given Harriet hopes of marrying the local vicar, Mr Elton. Emma is upset that Mr Knightley is angry. But she is confident that her match-making skills will bring Harriet a better husband.

Emma makes a lot of mistakes and causes more problems than happy marriages. Because she is so busy trying to arrange other people's lives, she nearly gives up her own chance of happiness. When she meets Frank Churchill, she decides that she should marry him. She can not understand why Mr Knightley does not like him. But will she find out in time?

When Emma visits some neighbours, she learns that Jane Fairfax is coming to visit for three months. Emma has never liked Jane, who is very quiet and a little cold. When Jane hears a suggestion that Mr Knightley may want to marry Jane, Emma is shocked. She does not want to see her good friend marry that young woman. In fact, she does not want Mr Knightley to marry anyone at all. As a family friend, he has always been there for Emma, listening to her and giving her advice. But Jane has a secret that Emma knows nothing about. And Mr Knightley is already in love, but Jane does not realise this. Secrets and misunderstandings produce surprising results as the story nears its end. All is not what it first appears to be.

Austen's vicar, Mr Elton, behaves in ways that are surprising in a vicar. He marries a woman for her money and offends people with his views on social class. He can be rude and unkind when it suits him. Eventually, Mr Knightley discovers that the vicar is not such a sensible man after all.

Emma finally learns that she has been wrong about people. She discovers that a poor man can make a very good husband for a woman of his social class. She comes to realise that it sometimes takes a while to get to know people well. And more importantly, quiet people like Jane Fairfax and Mr Knightley have very good qualities. By getting to know these people better, Emma is richly rewarded.

Jane Austen, one of England's greatest writers, was born on 16 December 1775 in the village of Steventon in Hampshire. Her father, George Austen, was a vicar. Jane was the seventh of eight children, and her greatest friend was her only sister, Cassandra, who was two years older. Jane studied for a short time in Oxford in 1783, then in Southampton, and finally from 1785 to 1786 in Reading, Berkshire. She enjoyed reading and began writing her first book in 1789. In 1801, her father stopped working, and the family moved to the fashionable town of Bath. People went to Bath to drink the waters for their health and to find husbands for their daughters. Jane didn't enjoy Bath very much; she was pleased to move back to Hampshire in 1809.

When Jane started writing, her father bought her a desk and

writing paper and he gave her his support. When he died in 1805, Jane with her mother and sister moved several times before moving into a house in Chawton, near Winchester. Jane felt very comfortable in this house with its large garden, beautiful country all round, and servants to do the housework. Jane's sister Cassandra never married, one of her brothers became a vicar, and two brothers went to sea on ships.

Jane's family was a loving one and also enjoyed parties, dinners and dances. Jane enjoyed playing the piano, like Emma Woodhouse in *Emma*. She received several offers of marriage but did not accept any of them. She lived quietly and spent much of her time writing. With help from her brother Henry, she found success with her first book, *Sense and Sensibility* (1811), which she wrote when she was twenty. Next came *Pride and Prejudice* (1813). Jane wrote both of these books some fifteen years before they appeared for sale. Two more books followed: *Mansfield Park* (1814) and *Emma* (1816).

Emma was the last book to appear before Austen's death and it did not bring her much money. Austen earned only about forty pounds for it. After her death, two other works, *Northanger Abbey* (1817) and *Persuasion* (1818) came out. At the age of forty-two, Jane became ill and was sent to Winchester, where she died.

Jane Austen's books describe, with a quiet but sharp sense of fun, a world she knew well: middle-class families with daughters in need of husbands. The perfect husband is young and handsome, loves music and literature, and is good at dancing. More importantly, he has plenty of money and a fine country house. Each book describes the guessing game of love between young ladies and gentlemen of the middle class of society. But in *Emma*, Austen's purpose is to remind the reader of the foolishness of match-making, which can bring about heart-ache rather than romantic love. While the subject of marriage is as old as man, Austen's style of writing brings a fresh eye to it. Her descriptions of people and their relationships are both honest and humorous. She listened to how people communicated and watched them very carefully. Then she took out her pen and paper and brought them to life on the page. Every word that she wrote had a purpose and was carefully planned. After finishing one of her books, it is a good idea for the reader to go back to the beginning and re-read some of the story. The reader will see that she knew exactly where her story was going and how it would end. In fact, many writers copied her style, but not all were as successful as she.

The wars in Europe at the time of these stories do not enter the picture. It was life inside the home that took first place in Austen's writing. It was a time when women did not go out to work but stayed at home and had children. Women obeyed their fathers until they married, and then they obeyed their husbands. When a husband died, they obeyed their sons and other relatives. They had a lot to do in the house – looking after children and servants. But when a wife died, another woman had to be found to take her place. A man had to have a woman to look after the children and teach them. Either a man would re-marry or he would employ a young woman who would live in the house with the family. If that were not possible, the children were given either to relatives or to richer people. This is what happened to Frank Churchill and Jane Fairfax in *Emma*.

When daughters were fifteen or sixteen it was time to find the perfect match and to get engaged. Families from the middle-class wanted to find husbands from families with as much money or more money than in their own. Parties and dances brought young people and their families together so they could look for the perfect match. It was usual for young women to play the piano in those days and they were asked to entertain at parties. Many of these young women tried to win a man's desire through her beautiful music. Love is an old story but a story that never grows old. Everybody is interested in who loves who and no one understood this better than Jane Austen.

The Austen's family home in Chawton, near Winchester in Hampshire, is now open to visitors. People come to see where she lived and to learn more about Jane Austen's family and her life. The desk at which she wrote is there, and is surprisingly small. Jane's mother and sister lie side by side outside the small church at Chawton, while Jane's body rests in the great church at Winchester.

A film of *Emma* was made for cinema in 1996, with Gwyneth Paltrow as Emma Woodhouse, Jeremy Northam as Mr Knightley, Sophie Thompson as Miss Bates and Ewan McGregor as Frank Churchill. A made-for-TV film of *Emma*, also in 1996, won two important prizes. Kate Beckinsale played Emma Woodhouse, Prunella Scales was Miss Bates and Mark Stong played Mr Knightley. Both films were very popular. Other stories by Jane Austen in Penguin Readers are *Pride and Prejudice*, *Sense and Sensibility* and *Persuasion*.

Chapter 1 An Offer of Marriage

Emma Woodhouse was beautiful, clever and rich. She lived sixteen miles from London in the village of Highbury and at nearly twenty-one years old she thought her life was perfect. But nothing stays the same for ever and even the most perfect life must sometimes change.

Emma was the younger of two daughters but only she lived with her father at the family home. Her sister Isabella lived in London with her husband and five children.

Emma's mother died when she was only five, and so her father found Miss Taylor to live with them at Hartfield and look after his two daughters. Miss Taylor became their teacher and friend and, even after Emma had grown up and didn't need Miss Taylor as a teacher any longer, she continued to live with them and was part of the family.

But Emma's comfortable life changed when Miss Taylor decided to get married to Mr Weston. Although his house – called 'Randalls' – was very near Emma's, she soon realised there would be a great difference between a Miss Taylor at Hartfield and a Mrs Weston half a mile from Hartfield. And so Emma and her father were left alone together, both wishing that Miss Taylor was still there too.

'What a pity Mr Weston ever thought of Miss Taylor,' said Mr Woodhouse, sadly.

'I cannot agree, Papa. They are very happy together, and I am happy for them. And we shall see them often. They will come here to Hartfield and we shall visit them at Mr Weston's house. We shall always be meeting.'

But although Emma tried to make her father feel happier, she was just as sad as him.

1

As they sat together playing cards on the evening after Miss Taylor's wedding, their friend Mr Knightley came to visit them. His brother John was Isabella's husband and he had just returned from their home in London.

'How was the wedding? Who cried the most?'

'Everybody was on time and looked their best,' said Emma, 'And there were no tears.'

'But I know how sad you must feel, Emma,' said Mr Knightley.

'Yes, but I am happy that I made the match myself, four years ago. People said Mr Weston would never marry again, but I saw the possibility of love,' said Emma.

'And now Miss Taylor has left us,' said Mr Woodhouse. 'So please do not make any more matches that might break up our circle of friends and family, Emma.'

Mr Knightley did not agree with Emma.

'I cannot see why you think you succeeded. It was no more than a lucky guess,' he said.

But Emma would not listen. She was sure it was because of her help that Miss Taylor had married Mr Weston, and now she had the idea of making another match.

'Mr Elton, the vicar – he is such a good and handsome man, everybody says so. And today, in the church, I could see that he would like it very much if it was *his* wedding. I wish I could help to find him a wife.'

'Leave him to choose his own wife,' laughed Mr Knightley. 'He is twenty-seven and can take care of himself.'

♦

Mr Woodhouse often invited his neighbours to Hartfield for an evening spent playing cards. Emma was happy to entertain their friends, although many of them were closer in age to her father than to her. But on one of these evenings Emma was luckier because one of their neighbours brought a young friend with her.

Seventeen-year-old Harriet Smith had been a pupil at the school in Highbury and was still living there with the head teacher because she had no living family. Harriet was very pretty and she and Emma immediately became friends. Harriet was very impressed. She thought Emma was wonderful and the surroundings of Hartfield were much better than she was used to. Emma liked Harriet a lot and wanted to introduce her into good society, but first she would have to help by teaching Harriet a few things. She decided this was a very kind and thoughtful plan.

After that evening, Harriet spent a lot of time at Hartfield and she and Emma were often together. Harriet told Emma about her schoolfriend Elizabeth Martin and her family, who she had stayed with in the summer. Emma heard about the Martins' farm and as she listened she began to realise that Mr Robert Martin was not the father of the family, but the son. And he was single.

'Tell me about Mr Robert Martin,' Emma said and Harriet did tell her. He was kind and clever, she said, and she liked him a lot. Emma thought a farmer was a most unsuitable friend for Harriet and knew Mr Elton, the vicar, would be a much better husband. She turned their conversation away from Robert Martin.

'If you compare him to other young men you will certainly see a difference. For example, Mr Elton is a perfect gentleman. Did I tell you what he said about you the other day?' she asked, and told Harriet how beautiful he thought she was. Harriet was very pleased and suddenly seemed to want to talk less about Mr Martin.

'I think Mr Elton likes you a lot. Remember how he wanted me to paint a picture of you? And how he sighed over it when I had finished?'

The painting had been Emma's idea at first but when he heard about it, Mr Elton was immediately enthusiastic and thought it a very good suggestion. Emma painted Harriet in the garden and

Mr Elton wanted to watch. But he walked about so much and asked so many questions that it became difficult for Emma to think about painting and for Harriet to think about standing still. Finally, Emma asked him to sit down and read something to them.

When the picture was finished Mr Elton thought it looked exactly like Harriet, but not everyone agreed.

'The picture is a little too beautiful around the eyes,' said Mrs Weston.

'Not at all!' replied Mr Elton. 'Miss Smith is just as beautiful as Miss Woodhouse has painted her.'

Mr Knightley knew Emma very well and was always honest with her. He said, 'You've made her too tall, Emma.'

'Oh, no,' said Mr Elton. 'Not too tall. Exactly right in my opinion.'

That was when Emma first began to see the possibility of a match between them and had great hopes that it would happen. Then Harriet had started talking about Robert Martin and Emma worried that he might spoil her match-making plans.

The next day she met Harriet in Highbury village and heard some unwelcome news.

'Miss Woodhouse,' said a very excited Harriet, 'Mr Martin has written to ask me to marry him!'

She showed Emma the letter and she agreed it was certainly a very good letter.

'So good that I wonder whether his sister helped him to write it,' she said.

'How shall I reply?' Harriet asked.

'I cannot tell you – it must be your own letter,' Emma replied. 'But I am sure you will write it so that he will not be too unhappy.'

'So you think I should refuse him,' said Harriet sadly, looking down.

That was when Emma first began to see the possibility of a match between Harriet and Mr Elton.

'I shall not advise you. This is something you must decide yourself.'

Harriet was silent. She looked at the letter again. 'I had no idea he liked me so much,' she said.

Emma decided she must speak to save Harriet from an unsuitable marriage.

'Harriet, if you doubt your answer, of course you should refuse him. If you cannot say "yes" immediately you must say "no".'

'Then I will refuse. Do you think I am right?'

'Perfectly, dearest Harriet. And remember, Mr Martin is only a farmer – he is not your equal or mine. If you married him, I could never visit you,' said Emma.

Harriet's letter was written and sent. She was a little quiet all evening and once she said she hoped Mr Martin and his sisters were not too sad. Emma tried to help her and started talking about Mr Elton again.

'We shall see him tomorrow, Harriet. He will come into this room and look at your picture again, and sigh as he always does when he sees it.'

Harriet smiled and became happier.

♦

When Mr Knightley and Emma were in the gardens at Hartfield the next day he spoke to her about Harriet.

'I congratulate you, Emma. She was always a pretty girl but you have taught her a lot. I think your friend may get some news today that will make her happy.'

When Mr Knightley and Emma were in the gardens at Hartfield the next day he spoke to her about Harriet.

Emma thought at first that Mr Elton might have said something to Mr Knightley but then he continued.

'Robert Martin asked my opinion of her, was she too young to marry? Was it too soon to ask her? I advised him to ask. He's very much in love with her.'

'He has already asked,' said Emma, 'and she has refused him.'

'What? She is a very foolish girl. Are you sure?'

'Of course, I saw her answer.'

Mr Knightley became angry with her.

'Saw it! You mean you wrote it! I think this was your idea, Emma.'

'It was not, but I believe that, although he is a very pleasant young man, he is not Harriet's equal.'

'Harriet Smith has no family and no money. This was a good match for her. Until she met you, she thought of nothing better for herself, but you have filled her head with ideas of high society and of how beautiful she is. She was happy enough with the Martins in the summer.'

Emma was unhappy because he was so angry with her, but she would not agree that she had been wrong.

'Now she knows what gentlemen are, she sees him differently. Now she is looking for something better.'

'Remember, Emma, sensible men do not want silly wives. Harriet may not have another chance to marry,' he replied. He started to walk away from her.

'And if you were thinking of Mr Elton for Harriet, it will not work. He is a good vicar and a good man but he will look for money and good family in a wife.'

Emma laughed. 'I am not trying to make a match for Harriet with Mr Elton,' she said, hoping that Mr Knightley would stop being angry and stay.

'Believe me, Emma, Mr Elton will choose sensibly,' he said over his shoulder. 'Good morning to you.'

Chapter 2   A Second Offer

Mr Knightley was so angry that it was some time before he went to Hartfield again. When Emma saw him again she could see that he had not forgiven her and she was sorry about that.

But she thought her plan was succeeding. Every time Mr Elton met Harriet and Emma he sighed a little more and Emma was certain he really did love Harriet.

Harriet was making herself a little book of poems, and some of the people she knew had suggested their favourites for the book. One day Emma told Mr Elton about it and then she said, 'Perhaps you could write something for Harriet's book? You are so clever it will be easy for you.'

'I'm sure I couldn't do it,' he replied, but the next day he called at Hartfield and left a paper with a short poem written on it. It was addressed to Miss —.

'He means it for you of course,' said Emma.

They read the poem together and saw that it was a very pretty love poem. Harriet was delighted with it.

'Mr Elton! He really is in love with me!' she sighed.

The poem was read to Mr Woodhouse and he said it was probably the best they had found. Then he started talking about Isabella.

'She is coming next week, and they will all be here for Christmas.'

'We must ask Mr and Mrs Weston to dinner while they are here, Papa. And Harriet must come as often as she can,' said Emma. 'You will love my nieces and nephews,' Emma said to Harriet, 'and it will be a Christmas to remember.'

♦

The next day, Emma had to visit a poor sick family in the village and Harriet went with her. The road to their little house passed the church and then later Mr Elton's house and for a moment they stopped to look at it. It was the first time Harriet had seen where Mr Elton lived.

'What a sweet house!' said Harriet.

'And there you and your book of poems will go one day. Then I shall often walk this way,' replied Emma.

They continued their walk and visited the family. Emma was a very kind young lady and she took them food and clothes for the children and tried to help as much as she could.

As they started their walk back to Hartfield, they met Mr Elton just as he was coming out of his house and he asked if he could walk with them.

Emma wanted to let Harriet and Mr Elton walk together without her and so she stopped and bent down to check her boot. They walked on and seemed to be having an interesting conversation. Emma tried to keep a long way behind but soon they stopped, turned and waited for her to catch up with them. She had hoped Mr Elton might take the opportunity to tell Harriet he loved her, but he didn't.

'He is very careful,' she thought. 'He will not tell her until he is sure she loves him.'

But although she did not succeed with that plan, she was certain they had moved a little closer to the great day of their marriage.

◆

Isabella, John Knightley and their children arrived at Hartfield the week before Christmas. Mr Woodhouse was delighted to see them all again and the family were happy to be together. They talked about their friends in Highbury and of course they talked about Mr and Mrs Weston.

'Do you see Mrs Weston often?' asked Isabella.

'Not as often as I would like, and she always goes away again,' said Mr Woodhouse sadly.

'But remember poor Mr Weston! She must go now that she is married, Papa,' laughed Emma.

'And what about the young man, Mr Weston's son? Has he been to see his father since the wedding?' asked John Knightley.

Everyone in Highbury knew about Mr Weston's son, Frank, but nobody had seen him. Several times he had said he was coming but each time something had happened to stop the visit.

Frank's aunt and uncle, Mr and Mrs Churchill, had adopted him when his mother died. He was only a baby and it seemed to Mr Weston at the time that it was the best thing to do. The Churchills had no children of their own and Frank took their family name. But Mrs Churchill was very jealous and wanted to keep Frank for herself. Although Frank saw his father once a year in London, he had not yet met his new wife.

If Frank Churchill finally did come to Highbury it would be very exciting for Mr and Mrs Weston, and for the whole village. Everybody looked forward to meeting him, especially Emma.

Mr Woodhouse told Isabella, 'I have seen a letter he wrote to Mrs Weston and he seems a very pleasant young man. I am only sorry he is not here now, so that you could meet him, my dear.'

◆

Mrs Weston invited all the family to Randalls for dinner on Christmas Eve★ and Harriet, Mr Knightley and Mr Elton were asked to join them. Two carriages were going from Hartfield and Mr Woodhouse arranged to meet Mr Elton at his house and take him to Randalls with them.

The day before, Harriet became ill with a cough and a bad throat and so she could not go. Emma explained to Mr Elton and he said he was very sorry that Harriet was ill. Emma thought he

★ Christmas Eve: The day before Christmas Day – December 24th

10

might be so unhappy that he would not go to Randalls without Harriet but he surprised her.

'It is a pity our friend cannot join our little party but I am looking forward to the evening,' he told her. 'We must hope she will soon feel better.'

Emma thought it strange that he was not more worried but she said nothing. During the journey, he was quite happy and even joked a little. He seemed to have forgotten poor Harriet and was obviously enjoying himself.

When they arrived at Randalls, Emma was surprised to find Mr Elton at her side most of the time. She heard Mr Weston telling the others something about Frank, but because Mr Elton was talking to her she could not hear everything.

Emma had an interest in Frank Churchill, although she had never met him. They were about the same age and because their two families were now joined in marriage it seemed to her that he was the man she should marry. She thought Mr and Mrs Weston had probably had the same idea, perhaps her father also.

At dinner she was sitting next to Mr Weston, and far from Mr Elton, so she had a chance to ask about Frank.

'I should like to see two more people here tonight – your friend Miss Smith and my son,' he said. 'Did you know we had another letter from him this morning? He will be with us in a fortnight. Mrs Weston doubts it, but I am sure he will come this time.'

'If you think he will come, I shall think so too,' said Emma. She hoped he was right because she wanted to meet Frank very much.

The evening at Randalls was a very pleasant one and, as they left for home, it started to snow.

Mr Woodhouse, Isabella and John all rode in the first carriage, and so Emma and Mr Elton were alone in the second. They had just driven through the gates and reached the road when

The evening at Randalls with the Westons was
a very pleasant one.

suddenly Mr Elton jumped up from his seat to sit next to Emma and took her hand in his. She immediately moved across the carriage.

'Mr Elton! What are you thinking of? Please stop this minute!' cried Emma, afraid that he had drunk too much of Mr Weston's excellent wine. But Mr Elton would not stop. He said he loved her and he would die if she refused to marry him. Again he moved next to Emma and again she moved away.

'I cannot understand this,' said Emma. 'Surely it is Miss Smith you love, not me!'

'Miss Smith? How can you think that?' he asked.

'But the painting – and the poem. Explain yourself, Mr Elton.'

'Miss Smith means nothing to me. I thought the artist was

wonderful, not the subject. And the poem was for you.' Mr Elton tried to take Emma's hand again. 'Miss Smith is a pretty, pleasant girl and I wish her well, but my visits to Hartfield have been for you only.'

Emma was so surprised that she did not know what to say. Mr Elton tried to take her hand again.

'Your silence makes me think that you always understood me,' he said.

'Then I see we have both made a mistake. I do not wish you to have any interest in me, Mr Elton, and I do not intend to marry anyone at present.'

After that they sat silently until the carriage stopped outside Mr Elton's house and he got out. They both said a cold 'good night' and the carriage drove Emma home to Hartfield, where the family were waiting for her.

Chapter 3   Mr Elton's Choice

That night it was difficult for Emma to sleep. For herself, she did not worry about what had happened in the carriage with Mr Elton, but she felt very sad for Harriet.

'Harriet has grown to like this man and then to love him,' she thought, 'and it was because of me.'

She remembered what Mr Knightley had said to her about him, that day in the garden. 'Mr Elton will choose sensibly,' he had said, and now it seemed he was right. He had not wanted Harriet, had never thought about her as a wife. All the time it had been Emma he wanted. But she knew the first and worst mistake had been hers. It was wrong and foolish to try to bring two people together and she was ashamed of herself.

'It was enough that I talked her out of love with Mr Martin. There, at least, I was right,' she thought.

13

The next day, Emma was pleased to see a lot of snow outside. This was a good thing because it meant she could not go to church and see Mr Elton, or go to visit Harriet, and none of them could meet. The snow stayed for several days after Christmas and the only visitor to Hartfield was Mr Knightley.

As soon as the snow disappeared, Isabella, John and the children went back to London. The same evening, a letter arrived for Mr Woodhouse from Mr Elton. It said he was leaving Highbury the next day and going to Bath to spend a few weeks with friends. There was no message in the letter for Emma and she was a little angry about that, but also pleased he was going away. She knew the next thing she must do was to speak to Harriet and tell her everything.

Harriet cried, but she did not blame Emma at all for what had happened. They went back to Hartfield together and Emma tried very hard to make Harriet feel better, but she knew only time could help her to forget. Perhaps when Mr Elton returned they might all be able to meet without feeling embarrassed.

◆

Mr Frank Churchill did not come. He wrote a letter of excuse and in it he said, *I hope to come to Randalls quite soon.*

Both Mr and Mrs Weston were very sorry but they decided perhaps the spring was a better time to visit and maybe he could stay for a longer time then.

Emma gave Mr Knightley the news and blamed the Churchills, especially his aunt. Mr Knightley did not agree.

'If he wanted to see his father, he could come. He is twenty-three or -four – at that age it is not impossible. A short time ago he was in Weymouth, so he can leave the Churchills when he wants to,' he said.

'It may not be easy for him all the time. His aunt and uncle may need him at home. Why do you dislike him so much?' asked Emma.

'I neither like nor dislike him because we have never met. But I cannot understand why this is so difficult for him. He seems a very weak young man.'

'We shall never agree about that,' said Emma. 'Perhaps he is just a kind and gentle man. Perhaps he does not want to make his aunt unhappy.'

'He is certainly very good at writing letters and making excuses. But Mrs Weston must feel very insulted because he has not come to meet her.'

Emma knew Mr Knightley was becoming angry about Frank Churchill and she could not understand why.

'I believe he will come soon,' she said. 'And when he does, everyone in Highbury will be very excited. We are all interested and want to meet him.'

'Oh? I never think of him from one month to another,' was all Mr Knightley said.

◆

Emma and Harriet were out walking one morning and in Emma's opinion had talked enough about Mr Elton for one day. Harriet could not forget him and still loved to hear his name. They were near the house where some old friends lived and Emma decided a visit to them may help Harriet to think about other things.

Mrs and Miss Bates loved to have visitors and Emma did not call at their house as often as she knew she should. They were quite poor but there was always tea and cake and a warm welcome for their visitors. Miss Bates loved to talk and because her old mother was deaf she repeated conversations by shouting at her.

They were delighted to see Emma and Harriet and made them sit near the fire and have tea with them. They asked Emma about their old friend Mr Woodhouse and were happy when she said he was in very good health.

'Have you heard from Miss Fairfax recently?' asked Emma, hoping they had not just received a letter.

Jane Fairfax was Miss Bates's niece. Her parents had died when she was young and she had come to Highbury to live with her grandmother and aunt. But then, an old friend of her father's, a Mr Campbell, had offered to look after her and Jane had gone to live with his family. Mr and Mrs Campbell had a daughter the same age as Jane and they were a rich family, so Jane was very lucky. Mrs and Miss Bates were very sad when she left Highbury but they knew it was much better for her to live in London with the Campbell family. She wrote to her aunt and grandmother regularly, and sometimes came to stay with them.

Emma and Jane Fairfax were about the same age and they knew each other but they were never friends. Miss Bates liked to tell everyone in Highbury about Jane because they were generally interested in her. Only Emma was not interested. She was bored with Jane's letters and hearing all about her life, but Miss Bates was a very kind lady and she knew it was polite to ask.

'We had a letter just this morning. Jane is coming to stay next week.'

'How lovely for you! And how long will she stay?'

'For three months at least – and we are so excited, Miss Woodhouse,' said Miss Bates. 'I said we are very excited!' she shouted at her mother.

'The Campbells are going to Ireland and because Jane has had a bad cold recently she decided not to travel with them,' she explained. 'Now, let me read you the whole letter, Miss Woodhouse.'

But although she knew it was not polite to go so suddenly, Emma did not want to stay and hear the letter.

'I am so sorry, but we must go now,' she said. 'My father will be waiting for us.'

Emma and Harriet left the house, although Miss Bates tried

very hard to make them stay a few more minutes. They promised to return the next week when Jane was there, and Emma invited Mrs and Miss Bates to come to Hartfield with Jane for an evening of music.

♦

The evening at Hartfield was pleasant and everyone enjoyed the music. Mr Knightley was invited, also Harriet and Mr and Mrs Weston, so there was quite a big party. Both Jane and Emma sang and played the piano, but Jane was much better. Emma tried to make conversation with her but she always found it difficult because Jane was quiet and a little cold. She often seemed unfriendly and Emma did not know why.

As she tried to find something to say, she remembered Miss Bates telling her that Jane had spent some time the summer before in Weymouth.

The evening at Hartfield was pleasant and everyone enjoyed the music.

'Did you meet Mr Frank Churchill? I understand he was also in Weymouth last summer.'

'Yes, we were introduced,' said Jane.

'Tell me about him. Was he handsome?'

'People seem to think so.'

'And sensible? Interesting? Clever?'

But Jane told her nothing. 'It is difficult to say, we did not meet often. He is very polite,' was all she said. Emma was not at all satisfied with that, and disliked Jane more than before.

♦

The next day, the same news came to Hartfield from two different people, first Mr Knightley, then Miss Bates. Mr Elton was going to be married.

Emma was surprised, it was only four weeks since he had left Highbury.

'He is marrying a Miss Hawkins of Bath. That is all I know,' said Miss Bates. 'A new neighbour for us all Miss Woodhouse! My mother is so pleased!'

'We are all pleased, of course,' said Emma, without looking at Mr Knightley.

That afternoon Emma decided she must tell Harriet the news when she called, before she heard it from Miss Bates or someone else. But it started to rain and Harriet did not come at her usual time. When she arrived later, the first thing she said was, 'Oh, Miss Woodhouse, what do you think has happened?'

Emma thought at once that Harriet knew about Mr Elton, but it was a different story that she told.

'It started to rain as I was walking through Highbury so I decided to wait in one of the shops until the rain stopped. And who do you think came into the shop?'

Emma could not guess but she could see how excited Harriet was.

'Elizabeth Martin and her brother! I did not know what to do. I was sitting near the door and Elizabeth saw me immediately, but he did not because he was busy with the umbrella. Then they both went to the other side of the shop and I kept sitting there – I could not go away because of the rain. At last he saw me and they whispered together for a little and then, Miss Woodhouse, what do you think?'

Harriet stopped for breath and Emma said, 'I really do not know Harriet, do tell me.'

'They came across to me and we shook hands and stood talking for some time. Then I saw that the rain had nearly stopped so I said I must go.'

'And now here you are.'

'Miss Woodhouse, I did not want it to happen, but it was so nice to speak to them again. Did I do the right thing?' asked Harriet.

Emma thought about it. As Harriet was so pleased to see Mr Martin again she might not be too upset at the news about Mr Elton, so the meeting must be a good thing.

'You behaved perfectly, Harriet. Now it is over and, as a first meeting, it can never happen again.'

For some time Harriet could not talk about anything except the Martins and Emma was right. The news about Mr Elton did not shock her so very much after all.

Chapter 4   Frank Churchill Appears

Mr Elton returned to Highbury a happy man. It was not long before everyone knew about his future wife. Her name was Augusta Hawkins and she came from a family with money. Ten thousand pounds was the rumour in Highbury.

Emma only saw him once or twice before he went to Bath

again, but Harriet always seemed to see him, or hear his voice. Everyone said he looked very much in love and when she heard that, Harriet became more unhappy.

One day when they were shopping in Highbury, Emma and Harriet met Mr and Mrs Weston.

'We have just been sitting with your father,' said Mr Weston. 'We wanted to tell you the good news. Frank is coming tomorrow and staying for a whole fortnight. We had a letter this morning.'

'And we shall soon bring him over to Hartfield,' said Mrs Weston.

They were both very happy and Emma was delighted. She hoped Mr Elton might be talked about less when Frank Churchill arrived in Highbury and was looking forward to meeting him at last.

♦

The next morning, Emma was in her bedroom when she heard voices downstairs and when she walked into the drawing room, there sat her father with Mr Weston and his son. Mr Weston introduced her and explained that Frank had come a day earlier than they thought.

He was a very handsome man and he looked sensible and friendly. She felt immediately that she would like him. As they talked together, Frank asked Emma about herself and Highbury. Did she like walking and riding? Was it a pleasant society in Highbury? Did they have musical evenings? And dancing – were there balls? They talked about Mrs Weston and Frank said how much he liked her already.

Emma looked at Mr Weston and could see what he was thinking. He had wanted to see them as a couple.

After some time, Mr Weston said they must go because he had business in Highbury and Frank said he might spend the time visiting some people he knew a little.

'Miss Jane Fairfax and I met last summer in Weymouth. Do you know the family she lives with?'

Of course Mr Woodhouse was delighted to give Frank directions to find Mrs Bates's house.

'Miss Fairfax is a beautiful woman and a brilliant musician,' said Emma and Frank agreed but with a very quiet 'Yes.'

'Her aunt will talk to you without stopping,' she continued, 'but they will make you very welcome.'

And so they left, but the next morning Mr Frank Churchill went to Hartfield to see Emma again, this time with Mrs Weston. All three walked together into Highbury and had a very pleasant morning. The more Emma talked to Frank the more she believed Mr Knightley had been wrong about him.

They stopped to look at the Crown Inn, a hotel in Highbury, and Mrs Weston told Frank about the ballroom there. He was immediately interested, although Emma said it was not used for balls any more. Frank looked through the windows and said it was a beautiful room and should be used again.

'You must arrange it, Miss Woodhouse,' he said, and Emma laughed at the idea.

♦

Emma's good opinion of Frank was shaken a little the next day when she heard he had gone to London just to have his hair cut. There was nothing wrong with that, except that it did not seem very sensible. But generally, everyone in Highbury seemed to think Frank was a very good young man. Everyone except Mr Knightley. He was not surprised to hear about Frank's trip to London and said he thought it was a silly thing to do.

That evening, Frank returned to Randalls from London. He had had his hair cut and laughed at himself for doing it. He was not ashamed and Emma began to think there was nothing wrong in it after all.

There was other news in Highbury that was more important. Some neighbours, Mr and Mrs Cole, were going to hold a dinner party. The Coles had a large and beautiful house. There was always music there, and there might possibly be dancing.

On the night of the party, Emma's carriage arrived at the Coles' house behind Mr Knightley's.

'I am surprised to see your carriage,' she said, 'you usually walk or ride everywhere. But this is more suitable for a gentleman so now I shall really be very happy to walk into the same room with you!'

Mr Knightley laughed at her and they went in to the party together.

At dinner, Emma sat next to Frank and they talked together about society in Highbury. Jane Fairfax sat across the table from them, wondering what they were talking about. Emma wondered whether other guests thought she and Frank were a special couple. After dinner, when he joined the ladies in the drawing room, he came across the room and sat next to Emma again. She began to realise that his life with his aunt and uncle was very boring.

'We never see anyone new and never have parties. My aunt is often ill and it is difficult for her to let me go away from home on my own.'

Harriet and some other young ladies were invited to arrive after dinner and Emma was happy to see Harriet looking pretty and confident when she came into the room. Frank spoke to Jane for a short time and was polite and friendly to Miss Bates. Before he could get back to his seat next to Emma, Mrs Weston had taken it.

'I have just made a little plan,' said Mrs Weston. 'How do you think Miss Bates and her niece came here tonight?' she asked.

'I suppose they walked.'

'Exactly. I suddenly thought it was not a very good idea for Jane to walk home late on a cold night, so Mr Weston suggested to Miss Bates that we should take them in our carriage. But she

Jane Fairfax sat across the table from them,
wondering what Emma and Frank were talking about.

said Mr Knightley had already offered his. I wonder if that is why he used his carriage. You know he usually walks.'

'Yes, that is typical of him,' said Emma. 'You know how kind he always is.'

'But perhaps it is more than kindness. The more I think about it, the more I am sure that I have made a match between Miss Fairfax and Mr Knightley!'

'Dear Mrs Weston! How could you think of such a thing? Mr Knightley must not marry! Isabella's son should have the family house after him. No, no I cannot agree to Mr Knightley's marrying. And I am sure it is not at all likely to happen,' whispered Emma. 'And Jane Fairfax too, of all women!' she added.

'She has always been a favourite with him,' said Mrs Weston. 'And I cannot see anything unsuitable in the match.'

Emma would not listen. 'Mr Knightley does not want to marry. Why should he? He is happy by himself with his farm and his sheep and his library.'

'But if he really loves Jane Fairfax...'

'No, no, you are quite wrong. Believe me, this is not a good match, or a possible one,' Emma replied.

They talked a little more and then, when Emma looked around, she saw that Frank was sitting with Jane. At that moment, Mr Cole asked Emma to play the piano and sing. She agreed but after two songs she invited Jane to play. Emma sat down and looked across at Mr Knightley. He was listening very carefully to Jane, and Emma started to wonder about what Mrs Weston had said.

When Jane finished her songs somebody suggested dancing and the room was quickly prepared. Mrs Weston sat at the piano and immediately Frank took Emma's hand and led her to the centre of the room.

While the other couples were getting ready Emma looked round for Mr Knightley. She knew he did not like dancing and if he danced with Jane Fairfax, it might possibly mean something. But she saw he was talking to Mrs Cole and another man had asked Jane to dance.

Emma enjoyed dancing with Frank and was sorry that there were only two dances before someone said it was getting late and they all ought to go home.

Frank took Emma to her carriage.

'Perhaps it was a good thing we had to stop,' he said. 'Soon I would have had to ask Miss Fairfax and she does not dance as well as you. Dancing with you was wonderful,' he told her as they said goodnight.

Chapter 5   Mrs Elton Comes to Highbury

The evening at Mr and Mrs Cole's house had been a very happy one. Emma looked back on it and smiled and so did Frank

Churchill. He had enjoyed the dancing so much that all the next day he was thinking of how to arrange more.

When Mr Woodhouse and Emma called at Randalls the next evening, he told Emma his idea.

'The dancing we started at the Coles' could be finished here at Randalls,' he said, 'with the same people and the same musician – what do you think?'

They thought it was a good idea. Mr and Mrs Weston were happy to use their house and Mrs Weston said she would play the music as long as they wanted to dance. Together, they added up the number of couples and then looked at the size of the two rooms at Randalls that could be used.

'Five couples – is the room big enough?'

'Perhaps the other room . . .'

'Should we also invite Miss Cox? And Miss Gilbert? And her cousins?'

Soon the five couples had become ten and Randalls was certainly not big enough for that. If it was so crowded, nobody could dance, they decided.

Frank did not give up the idea though, and by the middle of the next day he was at Hartfield to suggest another plan to Emma and her father.

'What do you think of having our little ball at the Crown Inn?' he asked.

They discussed the idea and decided it was a possibility. The room was much bigger and there was another room for dinner.

'My father and Mrs Weston are at the Crown at this moment, looking at the rooms,' said Frank. 'They would like you to join them and give your opinion.'

Mr Woodhouse stayed at home but Frank and Emma went immediately to the Crown.

Emma and Mrs Weston thought the room was a little dirty

although Mr Weston and Frank did not agree. Someone suggested asking Miss Bates to come and look, and Frank went across to her house. Miss Bates and Jane came and looked at the rooms and listened to the plan. Yes, they agreed, the Crown was the best place for the dance and they all spent the next half an hour walking from room to room and talking about the ball.

The only other thing to arrange was that Frank must write to his aunt and uncle to tell them he was staying in Highbury for another few days.

As people heard the news about the ball they were very excited. Jane Fairfax told Emma she was looking forward to it and Harriet talked about it a lot. Mr Knightley was the only one of Emma's friends who did not seem interested.

Unfortunately, a few days before the ball a letter came from Mrs Churchill. She was very ill, it said, and Frank must return home immediately. Emma was very upset when she heard the news. All their plans for the ball were ended and Frank was going away.

He came to Hartfield to see Emma and her father before he left for home.

'Of all the most horrible things, saying goodbye is the worst,' he said to Emma. He looked very unhappy.

'You will come again,' she replied.

'But I cannot say when. I shall certainly try, and then we shall have our ball.'

'And now there is no time to say goodbye to Miss Bates and Miss Fairfax before you go,' said Emma.

'I did call there on my way here. Just for three minutes,' he said. 'My father will be here very soon and then I must leave immediately. Miss Woodhouse, it has been a wonderful fortnight. I shall think of you all and dear Highbury. Mrs Weston has said she will write with all the news, but until I can be here again . . .'

He stopped and looked at Emma and she thought, 'He must really be in love with me.'

He was just going to speak again when his father arrived with Mr Woodhouse behind him and there was only time to shake her hand and say goodbye before he left.

It was a sad change for Emma. They had met almost every day that Frank had been in Highbury and now Emma's life seemed very quiet. That night she wrote in her diary, *I suppose I am in love with him. I think about him a lot and everything is so very boring without him.*

Mr Knightley was not sorry to see Frank go, but he was sorry that Emma was upset.

'You have so few opportunities for dancing, Emma. You are really very much out of luck,' he said to her.

◆

That night she wrote in her diary, I suppose I am in love with him. I think about him a lot and everything is so very boring without him.

In time, Emma told herself she was only a little in love with Frank. She was happy to hear about him from Mrs Weston and see his letters but she was not really unhappy without him. Soon she thought of him as only a dear friend. In his first letter he had spoken about Harriet.

'Please say my goodbye to Miss Woodhouse's beautiful little friend.'

Now that Emma was not in love with Frank herself, a little idea started to grow in her mind. She told herself not to think about it because, after Mr Elton, she knew match-making was a dangerous thing. But once the idea had come into her mind, she could not completely forget it.

Almost as soon as Frank Churchill left Highbury Mr Elton and his new wife arrived and suddenly everyone was talking about them. Harriet was unhappy about meeting them and talked about it a lot.

They first saw Mrs Elton at church but soon after Emma decided she and Harriet must call on her at her home.

Emma did not really like Mrs Elton. She seemed a little too comfortable, in a new place with new people. She was not very elegant, Emma thought. She dressed well and was pretty, but she did not seem a lady.

When Mr Elton came into the room he looked very uncomfortable, but Emma thought it was really bad luck for him. He had married Augusta, he had wanted to marry Emma, and Harriet had wanted him to marry her. And now they were all in the same room at the same time.

The visit was short and, in time, Mr and Mrs Elton returned it by visiting Hartfield.

There, Mrs Elton talked a lot about her brother and sister and their house. She said it was a lot like Hartfield.

'This room is just like their drawing room! Do you agree

Mr E? And the gardens! When my brother comes to visit us, we must all come to see your gardens, Miss Woodhouse.'

Emma liked her even less than before and Mr Elton had very little opportunity to speak at all.

'Is there a musical society in Highbury, Miss Woodhouse? Do you play?' she asked.

Emma said she did.

'We must start a little music club. It will be so amusing, don't you think?'

Before she could answer, Mrs Elton continued, 'We have just come from Randalls. What lovely people Mr and Mrs Weston are! He is quite a favourite of mine already! Mrs Weston was your teacher, I think?'

Emma did not have time to reply.

'I knew that and so I was a little surprised to find that she is such a lady. And who do you think arrived while we were there?' she asked.

Emma could not think of anybody to suggest.

'Knightley! Knightley himself! Was it not lucky? A very good friend of Mr E's! And I like him already. Knightley is quite the gentleman.'

Happily, it was then time for Mr and Mrs Elton to leave. Emma could breathe again.

'What an awful woman,' she thought. 'A very rude woman. Knightley, she called him! A music club! And she was surprised that Mrs Weston was a lady! I do not like her at all.'

Mr Woodhouse was kinder.

'A very pretty young woman,' he said, 'but she speaks a little too quickly. It hurts the ear.'

'Dear Papa,' said Emma. 'You are too kind.'

♦

During the next few weeks, Emma did not see anything to change her opinion of Mrs Elton. She was rude and thought herself very important, but Mr Elton seemed happy and proud of her. Emma wondered whether it was just because of the ten thousand pounds. Mrs Elton seemed to know Emma did not like her so she stayed away from Hartfield. But she became very interested in Jane Fairfax and decided Jane needed her help as an introduction into good society. Emma felt very sorry for Jane, who was more elegant than Mrs Elton could ever be.

One afternoon at Randalls, Emma, Mrs Weston and Mr Knightley were discussing Jane.

'Why does she stay here so long?' wondered Emma. 'She could go home to the Campbells and I cannot understand why she prefers to be here month after month.'

'If she stays, she will have to see Mrs Elton a lot of the time and I cannot believe she will like that,' said Mrs Weston. 'But perhaps she likes to be away from her aunt and grandmother occasionally.'

Mr Knightley agreed. 'And if there is no other person to be with . . .' he said, looking at Emma.

'I know how much you like Jane Fairfax. Perhaps you like her more than you realise,' Emma said to him.

'Oh – I see what you are thinking of. I am sure Miss Fairfax would not have me if I asked her, and I am also sure I will never ask her,' he replied.

Mrs Weston touched Emma's foot with hers.

Mr Knightley continued. 'So, you have decided that I should marry Jane Fairfax, have you?'

'Not at all,' said Emma. 'You were angry with me before for match-making and I had no idea of trying it with you. You would not come and sit with us in this comfortable way if you were married.'

Emma thought Mr Knightley might be angry with her if he

Emma thought Mr Knightley might be angry with her if he thought she and Mrs Weston were match-making him with Jane, but she was surprised to see that he seemed a little amused by the idea.

thought she and Mrs Weston were match-making him with Jane, but she was surprised to see that he seemed a little amused by the idea.

'I like Jane Fairfax, of course. But I have never thought of being in love with her. Not once,' he said.

After he had left, Emma said to Mrs Weston, 'Now, what do you think about Mr Knightley marrying Jane Fairfax?'

'My dear Emma, I think he tries too hard to tell us he is not in love with her. I would not be surprised if he was. I may be right in the end,' Mrs Weston replied.

Chapter 6   The Ball at the Crown Inn

Everybody in Highbury wanted to entertain Mr and Mrs Elton. Dinner parties and evening parties were arranged for them and they had so many invitations that they rarely spent an evening at home.

Emma knew they must have a dinner at Hartfield for them or people might guess that she did not like Mrs Elton. It was easy to decide who to invite – the Westons and Mr Knightley, of course, but there must be an eighth person. This ought to be Harriet, but Emma was not surprised when she said she could not come and she understood exactly why. Poor Harriet did not yet feel comfortable with the Eltons.

So Emma was able to ask Jane Fairfax to be the eighth person at the dinner. She was glad she could do this because Mr Knightley's words had worried her. He had said that Jane spent time with Mrs Elton only because no other person asked her.

'This is very true,' thought Emma. 'And I am certainly guilty of it. I ought to have been a better friend and I will try harder now.'

Everyone replied to her invitations and said they could come, and there was one other surprise guest. Isabella's two eldest boys were coming to stay at Hartfield and Mr John Knightley was bringing them on the day of the dinner party. So Emma had one extra guest until she lost another. Mr Weston had to go to London on business and could not be there for the dinner but he hoped to join them later in the evening.

On the day of the party everyone arrived on time. Mr John Knightley and his sons had met Miss Fairfax that morning as they were walking home from Highbury, when it had just started raining.

'I hope you did not get too wet this morning,' he asked Miss Fairfax as they stood together in the drawing room.

'I only went to the Post Office,' she replied. 'I go every morning to fetch the letters.'

'When you have lived to my age you will know that no letter is important enough to get wet for!' he said.

Mrs Elton had been listening to the conversation. 'What is this I hear? Going to the Post Office in the rain! You must not do it again,' she said loudly, 'I will not let you. I shall speak to Mr E and he will ask the man who fetches our letters to deliver yours too.'

Jane looked embarrassed. 'You are very kind, but I enjoy the walk,' she said, but Mrs Elton would not listen.

'My dear girl, say no more about it. It is already arranged,' she said.

'I really cannot agree to it. There is no need to make more work for your servant,' replied Jane.

Emma heard all this and wondered who might be writing to Jane, but she said nothing.

Dinner was ready. Emma took Jane's arm and they walked into the dining room together as if they were the best of friends.

Later, soon after the gentlemen had joined the ladies in the drawing room, Mr Weston arrived. He had only just come home from London and then walked to Hartfield.

After he had spoken to all the guests he gave his wife a letter which had been waiting at Randalls when he arrived there.

'It's from Frank,' he said, mostly to Mrs Weston, although everyone in the room was listening, 'and he's coming here next month! The Churchills are going to stay in Richmond for a few months – only nine miles from here! So he can be with us very often. He says we must start planning the ball again!'

Mrs Weston was very pleased and Emma was a little surprised to feel so excited by the news. Her guests said they were looking forward to seeing Frank again. Mrs Elton had never met him but she still had something to say.

'How delightful for him to come back to Highbury now there is a new neighbour to meet,' she said.

♦

Emma thought about Frank after the party and hoped that he might perhaps come back to Highbury less in love with her than before. She knew she must look carefully to see if this was true, then she could decide how to behave. She did not have to wait long.

As soon as the Churchills arrived in Richmond, Frank rode to Highbury for the day. He was certainly very pleased to see Emma, but she was sure he loved her less. He was as happy to talk and laugh as always, but after only fifteen minutes at Hartfield he hurried away to see other friends in Highbury.

This was his only visit for ten days, although he wrote to Mrs Weston and said they must now decide on a date for the ball and he would certainly be there.

♦

The day of the ball came. Emma and Harriet travelled together to the Crown Inn and arrived just after the group from Randalls. Frank was obviously happy to be with Emma again but he spent a lot of time walking to the door and back and listening for the sound of other carriages.

Soon some friends of Mr Weston's arrived, then Mr and Mrs Elton. Somebody said it was raining and Frank immediately went to look for umbrellas.

'We must not forget Miss Bates,' he said. 'I will see that she does not get wet,' and he went to the door and waited there. He soon came back with Miss Bates and Jane Fairfax.

'So very kind,' said Miss Bates. 'Not enough rain to worry about, but we must think of Jane, of course . . . well!' she stopped as she saw into the ballroom. 'Well! This is certainly brilliant!

An excellent room now that we have these wonderful lights!'

When everyone had arrived, Mr Weston and Mrs Elton led them forward for the first dance. Emma was delighted to see so many people dancing and knew she was going to enjoy the evening, but she was sad to see that Mr Knightley did not dance. He stood with some of the older men and looked quite serious except when Emma caught his eye and then he smiled at her. She thought it was a pity he did not like either dancing or Frank Churchill a little better.

The last two dances before dinner had almost started and Harriet had no partner. She was the only young lady sitting down. Until then, the numbers had been equal and Emma could not understand what had happened, but then she saw Mr Elton walking about. He would not ask Harriet if he did not have to and Emma thought he might suddenly escape into the card room. But she was wrong.

Mr Elton stood in front of the place where Harriet was sitting and talked to other people, but he did not even look at her. Emma was quite near and when Mrs Weston came and spoke to him she heard every word.

'You are not dancing, Mr Elton?' she asked.

'I certainly will, if you will dance with me.'

'Me! Oh no, I was thinking of a better partner for you.'

'Ah! Mrs Gilbert! Well, I am an old married man now and my dancing days are almost over, but I will be happy to dance with her,' he said.

'Mrs Gilbert does not dance, but there is a certain young lady – Miss Smith is not dancing,' Mrs Weston explained.

'Miss Smith,' he said, 'I did not see her. If only I were not an old married man! But I must be excused, Mrs Weston. I am afraid my dancing days are over.'

Mrs Weston said no more and Emma felt angry and upset for Harriet. She saw Mr Elton walk away and watched him and his wife smile at each other.

The next time Emma looked she saw a happier sight as Mr Knightley led Harriet to the dance. Emma felt very grateful to Mr Knightley and when she looked for Mr Elton she saw him going into the card room and hoped he felt foolish.

Emma did not have an opportunity to talk to Mr Knightley until after dinner.

'They wanted to hurt both you and Harriet,' he said. 'Why are they your enemies?'

'They cannot forgive me because I wanted Mr Elton to marry Harriet,' she replied. 'You were right about Mr Elton. I made a serious mistake,' she said.

'I think he has made a bigger one,' he replied. 'Harriet has some excellent qualities and she is very pleasant and easy to talk to. Unlike Mrs Elton!'

The next time Emma looked she saw a happier sight as Mr Knightley led Harriet to the dance.

At that moment Mrs Weston called them in to start the dancing again. 'Come, Emma, they are all lazy! You must start!'

'Who is your partner?' Mr Knightley asked Emma.

'You, if you will ask me,' she replied. 'We are not exactly brother and sister after all!'

'Brother and sister – certainly not,' he said, and they walked into the ballroom together.

Chapter 7   The Trip to Box Hill

Dancing with Mr Knightley was one of Emma's favourite memories of the ball. She was also glad they both thought the same of Mr and Mrs Elton and their insult to Harriet. It seemed as if Harriet's eyes had suddenly opened at the ball and she now saw Mr Elton differently. Emma walked in the garden the morning after the ball and decided it would be a happy summer – Harriet out of love, Frank not too much in love and Mr Knightley not arguing with her!

Frank was not going to call at Hartfield that morning because he had to go straight back to Richmond. So, as Emma was just going back into the house, she was very surprised to see him coming through the gates, with Harriet. Harriet looked white and frightened and he was obviously trying to calm her. Soon they were all in the house and Harriet immediately fainted.

Emma fetched some water and slowly Harriet became a little better and was able to tell her story.

She had been out with a friend and they were walking along the Richmond Road, when they suddenly met a group of gipsies. A child asked the girls for money and they were both very frightened. Harriet's friend ran away, but before Harriet could follow her, more gipsy children arrived and were all round her. She thought if she gave them some money they would go away but the opposite happened and suddenly she was surrounded by a lot of gipsies.

At that moment, Frank came along the road on his way back to Richmond. He saw what was happening, saved her and brought her to Hartfield. When he was sure Harriet felt better, he continued on his journey home.

In half an hour, the news was all over Highbury and everyone heard what had happened. Mr Knightley went with some other men to find the gipsies but they had already gone. The story soon became unimportant, but Emma remembered how worried Frank had been about Harriet and how she had held onto his arm. She began to have stronger hopes for them both.

About a fortnight later, Emma and Harriet were talking together and Emma said something about people getting married. To her surprise, Harriet replied, 'I shall never marry.'

'I hope this is nothing to do with Mr Elton,' replied Emma and Harriet denied it at once.

'No, of course not. It is someone much better.'

Emma understood at once. Harriet meant Frank Churchill and she was unhappy because she knew he came from a very good family and could not think of marrying her.

'I am not surprised about this Harriet. The way he saved you was enough to warm your heart, but you are right. You must not hope for too much.'

'He was wonderful, Miss Woodhouse! When I remember how I felt at the time – and then I saw him coming towards me. Suddenly I was happy again,' said Harriet.

'But strange things have happened before, Harriet. You must see how he behaves with you to know how much he really likes you. We made a mistake before because we hoped for too much. This time we will be more careful and not even speak his name,' said Emma.

◆

Mr Knightley had never liked Frank Churchill and as time went on he disliked him more. He began to think that, while Emma seemed to be his special favourite, he also had a liking for Jane Fairfax. Nothing was said to make him think this, but once or twice he had seen a certain look pass between them. Emma was his dear friend and he knew he must say something to her about it. She did not believe it at all and was amused by the idea so he said no more, but it worried him.

In June, a trip was arranged by Mrs Elton to Box Hill, a beautiful place in the countryside. It was going to be a simple party with only one or two servants and a picnic. A few days before the trip, one of the Eltons' carriage horses hurt his leg and they could not go.

'Most annoying, Knightley,' Mrs Elton said. 'What can we do? The weather is perfect too.'

'Come and eat my strawberries. They are ready now and you do not need horses to travel that distance.' He meant it as a joke but Mrs Elton thought it was a delightful idea.

'Excellent!' she said. 'I will arrange food and guests. Just name the day.'

Mr Knightley certainly did not want her to arrange anything and said he could do it himself.

'Very well. I shall bring Jane and her aunt and you can ask the other guests. We will walk around your gardens, pick strawberries and sit under trees, just like a gipsy party! It will be very pleasant.'

As Emma walked in Mr Knightley's gardens on the day of the party she saw him and Harriet standing together away from the others. She was a little surprised, but pleased to find them in conversation. She joined them and they walked together for a time.

Mr Weston had invited Frank but by lunch time he still had not arrived and Mrs Weston began to be worried about him. They all had lunch in the house and then afterwards went into the garden again. Still there was no sign of Frank. Emma stayed in the drawing room with Mr Woodhouse for a time because it was too hot for him to be outdoors. She was just walking through the hall when Jane Fairfax suddenly came in through the door. She looked as if she wanted to escape from something and she was surprised to see Emma.

'Will you be so kind,' she said, 'when they ask about me, to say I have gone home? My aunt does not realise how long we have been here and I think I should go back to see my grandmother now.'

It was a long walk to Highbury and Emma wanted to order her carriage, but Jane did not want this. 'I would like to walk,' she said as she left.

Not long after, Frank arrived. His aunt had been ill again, he said. He was quite annoyed because he had not been at the party and Jane had already gone home.

The Eltons' horse was better and they had already decided to make their trip to Box Hill the next day.

'You must come with us,' Emma said to Frank, who was still a little angry. At first he said he did not want to ride from Richmond again the next day, but then changed his mind and said to her, 'If you wish me to join the party, I will.'

♦

It was a wonderful sunny day for the trip to Box Hill and it should have been a happy party, but it was not. They separated too much into groups – the Eltons walked together, Mr Knightley went with Miss Bates and Jane, and Frank looked after Emma and Harriet. Mr Weston tried all day to make them come together but he could not.

Emma was bored. She had never seen Frank Churchill so silent and stupid. He said very little and did not seem to listen to anything she said, and Harriet was quiet because he was quiet.

When they all sat down together for their picnic lunch it was better. Frank became much happier and more amusing, and Emma thought he was trying very hard to win her heart. They talked and laughed together, although the rest of the group did not join in.

'We are the only people speaking,' she whispered to him. 'It is silly for us to entertain seven silent people.'

'What can we do to make them talk?' whispered Frank. Then he had an idea.

'Ladies and gentlemen, I am ordered by Miss Woodhouse to say that you must each say something to entertain her. You can say one very clever thing, two quite clever things or three very boring things, and she promises to laugh at them all!'

'Oh, well,' said Miss Bates, 'then I need not worry. I shall be sure to say three very boring things as soon as I open my mouth!'

Emma could not stop herself. 'But there may be a difficulty – you can only say three things, no more.'

Miss Bates did not immediately understand, but when she did,

When they all sat down together for their picnic lunch
Frank became much happier and more amusing, and Emma thought
he was trying very hard to win her heart.

she looked very hurt and embarrassed. The others were all silent.

'Ah, yes, I see what she means. I will try not to say more than three,' she said quietly.

Mr and Mrs Elton stood up and said they did not like games like that and they were going for a walk, and soon Mr Knightley, Jane and her aunt followed them. Frank became louder and more annoying until he began to give Emma a headache. When the servants came to say the carriages were ready she was quite pleased.

As Emma was waiting for her carriage, Mr Knightley joined her. He looked around to see if they were alone, then said, 'Emma, I must speak to you. How could you be so cruel to Miss Bates?'

Emma remembered and was sorry but tried to laugh about it.

'It was not so bad and she probably did not understand me,' she said.

'She certainly did. You were very rude to her and you have hurt her.'

'Miss Bates is a very good woman, but you know that she is also rather silly.'

'She is not your equal, Emma. She is not rich and clever like you and I was ashamed of you for speaking to her like that. And it was worse because you said it in front of other people. Badly done, Emma. Very badly done.'

Mr Knightley walked away to his horse and Emma climbed into her carriage. She felt angry with herself and ashamed. She thought she must say something to Mr Knightley and looked back, but he had already gone.

The journey home to Hartfield did not make her feel better. Harriet was tired and silent and as Emma remembered what she had said to Miss Bates, tears ran down her face.

Chapter 8   A Secret Engagement

Emma thought about the trip to Box Hill all evening. Maybe the rest of the party had enjoyed it, but she could only think of Miss Bates and how angry Mr Knightley had been with her. She knew she had been wrong and she was certain she would never do it again. She decided to call on Miss Bates the next morning.

Emma went early, and as she walked into the room she just had time to see Jane go out of the opposite door.

'We are very happy to see you, Miss Woodhouse,' Miss Bates said, although Emma thought her voice was not quite as friendly as usual. She asked about Jane.

'Poor Jane has an awful headache,' she told her. 'She has been writing letters all morning – to the Campbells and to her other friends. We shall be so sad when she goes, but it is a very good opportunity for her, you know.'

Emma was surprised. 'Where is Miss Fairfax going?' she asked.

'To a Mrs Smallridge – three delightful little girls to look after. An old friend of Mr Elton's. Jane will be just like Mrs Weston was to you and your sister. She finally decided to go yesterday evening when we were at Mrs Elton's house. A lovely evening, with good friends.'

'And when is she going?'

'Very soon, within a fortnight. My dear mother does not like to think about it,' said Miss Bates sadly.

Emma stayed a little longer and then walked home.

When she arrived Mr Knightley was at Hartfield and he seemed more serious than usual.

'I wanted to see you before I went away, Emma. I am going to London to spend a few days with John and Isabella. I have been thinking about it for some time.'

Emma thought he looked as if he had not forgiven her. He

stood, ready to go but not going, and Mr Woodhouse chose that moment to ask her how Mrs and Miss Bates were.

Mr Knightley suddenly appeared to be pleased with her. He took her hand and she at first thought he might kiss it, but he let it go again. Then he left immediately.

Emma felt happier now that they were friends again. Her father said he had been there for half an hour and she thought, 'What a pity I did not come home sooner!'

The next day brought news from Richmond. Mrs Churchill, Frank's aunt, had suddenly died. Mr and Mrs Weston were shocked and Emma wondered how Frank's life might change now. Perhaps he would be able to marry Harriet if he wanted to. Emma still hoped for this, but it was too soon to make any plans.

Emma's first wish at this time was not for Harriet but for Jane. She wanted to be a friend to her now, before it was too late and she went away to Mrs Smallridge.

She wrote to her and invited her to come to Hartfield for the day. Jane thanked her for her invitation but refused. Emma heard that she was not feeling well and thought an hour or two in the countryside might help, so she offered to call in her carriage one day. Jane replied that she was not well enough to go out, but when Harriet said she had seen Jane out walking only that morning, Emma had no doubt. Jane did not want any kindness from her, and she was very, very sorry.

♦

One morning, about ten days after Mrs Churchill had died, Mr Weston called at Hartfield and asked Emma to go back to Randalls with him. 'Mrs Weston must see you alone,' he said.

Emma could not guess what might be so urgent and when they arrived Mr Weston left them alone together.

'Frank has been here this morning,' said Mrs Weston. 'He came to talk to his father about something, a young lady he is in love with . . .'

Emma thought first about herself, then Harriet.

'. . . Frank and Jane Fairfax have been secretly engaged since they met in Weymouth last October,' she said.

Emma was very surprised.

'Jane Fairfax! So they were engaged before either of them came to Highbury!'

'And nobody knew about it. We are very upset by the way he has behaved, specially to you, Emma. We cannot excuse him for that.'

'You need not worry about me. When we first met I did think he was very attractive,' said Emma, 'And I thought I was in love with him. But for at least the last three months I have not felt at all like that.'

Mrs Weston was much happier then and called her husband into the room.

'It was our wish that you should love each other and we thought you did. Since this morning we have felt very upset for you,' she said.

'But he was very wrong. He might have made me love him, and what about Jane? She is going to Mrs Smallridge now. . .'

'He did not know about that, Emma. It was only when he found out that he decided to tell his uncle and then come here,' said Mr Weston. 'And Mr Churchill was happy with the match. While Mrs Churchill was alive there was no hope of them marrying, but now they can.'

'She will be a good wife for him,' said Emma. 'I congratulate you and them.'

Emma now had to do a difficult thing – tell Harriet before she heard about it in Highbury.

Harriet had just come home when Emma arrived.

'Miss Woodhouse – isn't the news very strange?'

'What do you mean? What news?'

'About Jane Fairfax and Frank Churchill. They have been secretly engaged and are now going to be married. I just saw Mr Weston and he said you already knew.'

Harriet certainly did not look upset, and Emma did not understand it.

'Did you ever suspect that he loved her?' asked Harriet.

'Of course not. I let you hope for him.'

'Me? I have never hoped for Frank Churchill!'

'Harriet, what do you mean?'

'I know we agreed not to speak his name, but I do not understand how you could have made this mistake. I spoke of someone much better than Frank Churchill.'

Emma sat down and tried to keep calm.

'Let us be very clear, Harriet. I remember you saying how you felt when he saved you from the gipsies – I am certain I did not imagine it.'

At first Harriet looked confused, then she said, 'I remember the conversation, but I was thinking of something very different at the time. The night of the ball when Mr Elton would not dance with me and there was no other partner in the room . . .'

'Good God!' cried Emma. 'You are speaking of Mr Knightley! This is an awful mistake.'

Harriet did not think so.

'He is kind and sweet to me. And you said yourself, strange things have happened before.'

Suddenly Emma realised why it was so much worse now that Harriet was in love with Mr Knightley and not Frank Churchill. It cut through her like a knife. She would be unhappy if Mr Knightley married anyone except herself!

The rest of the day and the next night she did not stop thinking about it. How long had she loved Mr Knightley? How could she be happy now without him?

He was coming back to Highbury very soon and until then, Emma decided, she and Harriet had better not meet.

Mrs Weston visited Jane Fairfax and she told Emma about it afterwards.

'She only decided to go to Mrs Smallridge because she believed Frank was in love with you and they could never marry. Now that she has spoken to him again and the secret is out, she will not go. She said you were very kind to her recently when she was ill,' said Mrs Weston.

'I am glad she is happy now, and very sorry if I sometimes hurt her in the past,' Emma replied.

That evening there was a storm and it continued all night. Emma sat quietly with her father and it reminded her of the evening of Mrs Weston's wedding day. Then Mr Knightley had walked in soon after tea and made them feel happier, but everything was different now. Mrs Weston had told Emma she was going to have a baby, so they were probably going to see less of her. Jane and Frank were getting married and might not live in Highbury, and if Mr Knightley and Harriet married she would also lose her two dearest friends to each other. There might not be other evenings when Mr Knightley just walked into Hartfield for the evening.

Emma felt very sad and could not sleep that night. The bad weather continued next morning but in the afternoon it stopped raining, the sun came out and it was summer again.

Chapter 9   Three Weddings

That afternoon, Emma was walking in the garden when she saw Mr Knightley come through the gate. She did not know he had returned to Highbury and she was thinking of him and Harriet at exactly that moment. She was beginning to believe he might really love Harriet and they may perhaps marry one day.

They talked about Isabella and John but Mr Knightley was quieter than usual. Emma wondered whether he wanted to talk to her about Harriet but found it difficult to know how to start. She tried to make conversation.

'We have some surprising news – a wedding.'

'Miss Fairfax and Frank Churchill. I have already heard about it,' he replied.

Emma immediately thought he had been to see Harriet before he came to Hartfield and she had told him. 'How is it possible that you know?' she asked.

'Mr Weston wrote to me on business and he told me the news in his letter,' he explained.

'You are probably not as surprised as we were. You suspected it before and tried to warn me.' Emma sighed. 'But I would not

They talked about Isabella and John but he was quieter than usual.

listen to you. I seem to have been blind about a lot of things.'

Nothing was said for a few minutes, then Mr Knightley took her hand and pressed it to his heart.

'Dear Emma, time will help you forget him,' he said, 'and he will soon be gone.'

'You are very kind, but you have misunderstood. I am sorry for things I did and tried to do, but I never loved Frank Churchill and he did not love me. He was only trying to hide his love for Jane and I just enjoyed being with him. It was not love,' said Emma.

There was suddenly a great difference in Mr Knightley. He held her hand tightly. 'Emma, might there be a chance for me?'

Emma was so surprised she could not speak.

'If your answer is "No" please tell me now, Emma. I cannot tell you everything I feel for you. If I loved you less I might be able to talk about it more,' he continued. 'But you know what I am, everything I say to you is true. And I tell you now, my dear, that I have always loved you.'

Emma had never been happier. She told him then that she loved him too. As they kissed she thought, just for a moment, of Harriet and was glad she had not said anything to Mr Knightley about her.

They went into the house and had tea with Mr Woodhouse but, for the present, said nothing to him about their love. After Mr Knightley had gone, Emma wrote to Isabella and suggested she invited Harriet to London. She thought it would be a good idea if Harriet went away from Highbury for a short time so they did not see each other for a few weeks.

Later that day, Mr Knightley returned to Hartfield. He wanted to ask Emma to marry him but he was worried that Mr Woodhouse would be very upset if Emma left Hartfield and went to live in Mr Knightley's house.

'I could not leave him,' said Emma.

'We could all live in my house,' he suggested.

As they kissed she thought, just for a moment, of Harriet and was glad she had not said anything to Mr Knightley about her.

'He would be very unhappy if he had to leave Hartfield,' said Emma.

'Then there is only one answer,' said Mr Knightley. 'We must all live in Hartfield.'

It was a good idea and Emma said she would think about it before speaking to her father. The more she thought about it, the more delightful the idea became. The only thing that made her sad was Harriet. If she was still in love with Mr Knightley, she could not be a part of the happy picture in Emma's mind.

Poor Harriet. Emma knew there was going to be a day when she could forget Mr Knightley, but it was not likely to be soon. It was too much to hope that even Harriet could be in love with more than three men in one year.

Harriet was invited to London as planned and, before Harriet left, Emma wrote to her and explained that she and Mr Knightley wanted to marry.

Mr Woodhouse's carriage took Harriet to Isabella's house and, after she had gone, Emma felt more comfortable. Now she could enjoy Mr Knightley's visits without feeling guilty. She was sure that Harriet could find interesting things to do and there may be people to meet in London to help her forget all that had happened.

Emma told her father she and Mr Knightley were going to get married and they were all going to live in Hartfield. Mr Woodhouse did not like changes in his life and at first he was a little shocked.

'We will always be here to look after you, Papa. Nothing will change for you, and you know how much you enjoy talking to Mr Knightley,' she said. Emma talked to him about it a little longer and he soon saw that they could all be happy together and it was really quite a good plan. 'Perhaps in a year or two . . .' he said.

The news spread quickly and generally people in Highbury thought it was a very good match, except for Mr and Mrs Elton. She had never liked Emma and thought it was terrible that they would all live together at Hartfield.

'It will not work. It is a shocking idea,' she said to her husband.

He just said, 'She probably always meant to catch Knightley if she could.'

♦

About two weeks later, Mr Knightley called at Hartfield one morning as usual and told Emma, 'I have something to tell you – some news.'

'Good or bad?' she asked.

'I think it is good, but I am afraid you will not agree with me. It is about Harriet Smith.'

Emma could not think what had happened to her.

'She is going to marry Robert Martin,' he said.

'Good God, that is impossible so soon . . . how do you know this?'

'Robert Martin told me himself, half an hour ago. You do not like the idea, I can see. But in time you will grow to like him as much as I do,' he said.

'I am not unhappy at all, just very surprised. Tell me the whole story. How did it happen?' asked Emma.

Mr Knightley told her he had sent Robert to London with a message for John, and at his house he met Harriet again.

'The family were going out together that evening and they asked Robert to join them. During the evening he told Harriet he still loved her and she agreed to marry him,' he said.

'I hope they will be very happy together,' said Emma, with a smile.

'Have you changed your mind about him?'

'I think I have. I hope so, because I was a fool before.'

'I have also changed my mind about her,' said Mr Knightley. 'I used to think she was a silly girl, but the more I talked to her the more I saw that she is kind and sensible. I sometimes thought you must wonder why I had suddenly started to spend time talking to Harriet,' he continued, 'but I wanted to get to know her and understand why you liked her so much. They will make a good match.'

Emma agreed and was very glad that her friend was now as happy as she was.

That afternoon, Emma and her father drove to Randalls. Mrs Weston was alone in the drawing room when they arrived but they had only just sat down when they saw a group of people in the garden.

'Frank arrived here this morning and he has just come back in the carriage with Miss Fairfax, her aunt and her grandmother. They are coming in now,' Mrs Weston said.

The little group came into the drawing room with Mr

'Frank arrived here this morning and he has just come back in the carriage with Miss Fairfax, her aunt and her grandmother.'

Weston, and Emma was very pleased to see Frank and Jane again. While the rest of the party talked together, Frank said to Emma, 'I am surprised you did not suspect us. Once, I nearly told you but I changed my mind. I hope you can forgive me for the way I behaved to you. I know I was wrong and I only did it because I could see you had no thoughts of marriage.'

'There is nothing to forgive,' she said. 'I also behaved badly.'

'I am delighted to see you again,' he said, 'and also to hear that you and Mr Knightley are engaged. You will be very happy, I am sure of it.'

◆

The next day, Harriet arrived back in Highbury and called on Emma immediately. She told her she felt a little foolish now when she thought of Mr Knightley, and Emma was pleased to see that she loved Mr Martin very much.

Very soon, Robert Martin was invited to Hartfield and Emma saw that Mr Knightley had been right about him. He was polite and kind and she had no doubt that Harriet was always going to be happy in his home surrounded by people who loved her.

♦

Before the end of September, Harriet and Robert Martin were married in Highbury church by Mr Elton – the last of the three couples to get engaged and the first to be married.

Jane Fairfax and Frank Churchill had planned their wedding for November and Emma and Mr Knightley thought October was a good time for theirs. Isabella and John were going to be staying at Hartfield at that time and they could look after Mr

The small group of true friends who were invited to the wedding were delighted by it and Emma and Mr Knightley were perfectly and completely happy.

Woodhouse while the couple went away to the sea for a fortnight.

The only problem was making Emma's father agree with them that October was a good time for the wedding. Mr Woodhouse thought it was too soon and suggested they wait a little longer but something happened to change his mind.

Mrs Weston's chickens were all stolen from the chicken house one night and the same thing happened to other people in Highbury. Mr Woodhouse was very worried about this. He said he would be nervous in his house after John and Isabella had gone back to London if there was no other man at Hartfield to look after him. John had to return to London by the end of the first week in November so it was finally agreed that the wedding must be arranged for October.

Emma and Mr Knightley's wedding was a simple one. Mrs Elton had not been invited and so her husband described it to her. She thought it sounded very plain and was nothing compared to her own wedding.

But the small group of true friends who were invited were delighted by it, and Emma and Mr Knightley were perfectly and completely happy.

ACTIVITIES

Chapters 1–2

Before you read

1 Look at the Word List at the back of the book and then answer these questions.

    a When two people get *engaged*, does this mean they intend to *adopt* or marry or use a *carriage*?

    b If you *suspect* someone of spreading *rumours* about you, are you *delighted*, *impressed* or annoyed?

2 Read the Introduction and answer these questions. What do you find out about:

    a Emma Woodhouse?

    b Jane Austen's books?

    c how middle-class families found husbands for their daughters?

3 Look at the pictures in Chapters 1 and 2. When do you think this story happens? Do you think Emma's family are rich or poor? Why?

While you read

4 Match these names with the descriptions.

    Emma Woodhouse   Isabella Woodhouse

    Miss Taylor   Mr Weston   Mr Knightley

    John Knightley   Mr Woodhouse   Mr Elton

    Harriet Smith   Robert Martin

    a .... husband of Isabella and brother of Mr Knightley

    b .... feels responsible for matching Mr Weston and Miss Taylor

    c .... Emma and Isabella's teacher, who is now Mrs Weston

    d .... Emma's father, who wishes that Miss Taylor had not married and left his house

    e .... Emma's friend who advises her not to try to find a wife for the vicar

f .... unmarried vicar, who wants Emma to paint a
picture of Harriet

g .... sister of Emma, who is married with five
children

h .... Emma's seventeen-year-old friend, who has no
family and no money

i .... a farmer, who is the brother of Harriet's friend
Elizabeth

j .... owns a house called Randalls

5 What does Emma think? Put a (✓) next to the correct answers.
Emma thinks that:

a Mr Elton is in love with Harriet. .....

b Harriet would like to become Mrs Elton. .....

c Frank Churchill, Mr Weston's son, will not be an
interesting visitor to Highbury. .....

d Mr Elton will not want to go to Randalls after he
hears about Harriet's poor health. .....

e she will marry Frank Churchill because she loves him. .....

f there has been a misunderstanding between her
and Mr Elton. .....

After you read

6 In Chapter 1, how does Emma feel about these people? Why?

a Mr Elton

b Robert Martin

c Harriet

d Mr Knightley

7 How does the relationship between these people change? Why?

a Miss Taylor and Mr Weston

b Harriet Smith and Robert Martin

c Emma Woodhouse and Mr Elton

Chapters 3–4

Before you read

8 Read the title of Chapter 3. What do you think Mr Elton will do
next? What will Emma tell Harriet, do you think?

9 Read the title of Chapter 4 and look at the pictures on pages 23 and 27. Do you think Emma will like Frank Churchill when she meets him? Why (not)? Will he like her?

While you read

10 Find the incorrect word in each sentence, cross it out and write the correct word.

a When Emma tells Harriet about Mr Woodhouse's feelings, she cries but does not blame Emma. ....

b Mr Knightley tells Emma that Mrs Weston must feel delighted because Frank has not come to visit her. ....

c Jane Fairfax lived with her aunt, Miss Bates, and her grandmother, Mrs Bates, after her parents died but later lived with a rich family in Highbury. ....

d After trying to get information about Frank Churchill from Jane, Emma likes Jane more than before. ....

e After Harriet meets Elizabeth Martin and her brother, Robert, Emma thinks the meeting is a bad thing. ....

11 Circle the correct word in *italics* in each sentence.

a When Emma meets Frank Churchill, she is *impressed / unimpressed* by his handsome face and friendliness.

b Emma tells Frank that Jane Fairfax is a *dull / brilliant* musician.

c Frank likes going to *balls / games* and is very interested in the ballroom at the Crown Inn.

d At the Coles' party, *Jane / Harriet* wonders what Emma and Frank are talking about.

e Emma is *pleased / worried* when Mrs Weston suggests that she has made a successful match between Jane and Mr Knightley.

12 Work with another student. Have this conversation.

> *Student A*: You are Emma. Your father has received a letter from Mr Elton about his plans to go to Bath with friends. You tell Harriet everything about Mr Elton.
>
> *Student B*: You are Harriet. You are in love with Mr Elton, and Emma's news about him is a terrible shock. Ask questions about him. Tell Emma that you do not blame her. Ask for advice.

13 How does Emma feel about these people?

> **a** Miss Bates **b** Jane Fairfax **c** Frank Churchill

Chapters 5–6

Before you read

14 Read the titles of Chapters 5 and 6 and answer these questions.

> **a** Who will Emma meet for the first time? Will she like this person, do you think? Why (not)?
>
> **b** What kind of place do you think the Crown Inn is?
>
> **c** What do people do at a ball?

15 What is Emma's opinion of Mrs Weston's match-making between Mr Knightley and Jane Fairfax? Why? Look at the picture on page 31 and read the sentence under it. How does Mr Knightley feel?

While you read

16 Write the correct word in these sentences.

After deciding that **(a)**........................ is not big enough for a ball with ten couples, Frank suggests that they have it at the Crown Inn. Then Frank writes to his aunt and uncle to tell them that he is staying in **(b)**........................ for another few days. Everyone is excited about the ball except **(c)**........................ When Frank receives a letter from **(d)**........................ he has to leave, and the plans for the ball are ended. Mr Knightley is not sorry to see Frank go. But he is sorry that **(e)**........................ is upset.

17 Put these events in the correct order. Write 1–7.

    a When Mrs Weston suggests that Mr Elton
       dance with Harriet at the ball, he rudely makes
       excuses and walks away.   .....

    b Mr Knightley tells Emma that Harriet is a better
       person than Mrs Elton.   .....

    c Jane will not allow Mrs Elton to arrange for
       Jane's letters to be fetched from the Post Office.   .....

    d Because Mr Elton and his wife want to hurt
       Harriet and Emma, Mr Knightley invites Harriet
       to dance with him.   .....

    e Emma invites Jane instead of Harriet to her dinner.   .....

    f In front of Emma's guests, Mr Weston shows
       Frank's letter to his wife and suggests they start
       planning the ball again.   .....

    g When Frank returns to Highbury for a day, Emma
       is satisfied that he loves her less.   .....

After you read

18 Discuss with another student:

    a Emma's change in attitude towards Frank Churchill.

    b the reason why Mr Knightley does not like Frank.

    c the reason why Emma dislikes Mrs Elton.

    d Mr Knightley's feelings for Jane Fairfax.

19 What is your opinion of Mr Knightley? Why?

Chapters 7–8

Before you read

20 Read the title of Chapter 7 and look at the picture on page 41. Where are they? What are they doing?

21 Do you think Harriet will fall in love again? Will Emma fall in love? Who will get secretly engaged in Chapter 8?

22 What happens? Put a (✓) next to the correct sentences.

   a Emma's favourite memory of the ball is her
      dance with Mr Knightley. .....

   b Harriet nearly faints when she tells Emma that
      the gipsies stole her money. .....

   c After Frank saves Harriet from the gipsies, Emma
      hopes that Frank will fall in love with Harriet. .....

   d Mr Knightley is worried that Frank likes Jane
      Fairfax more than Emma, but Emma does not
      believe it. .....

   e At Mr Knightley's house, Jane leaves the party
      and will not allow Emma to order a carriage for her. .....

   f Mrs Elton arranges a picnic at Box Hill and
      everyone has a delightful time there. .....

   g Mr Knightley is angry with Emma for being cruel
      to Mrs Elton. .....

23 Write the name of the person on the line.

   a Whose children will Jane Fairfax look after? ....

   b Who dies? ....

   c Who does not want any kindness from
      Emma? ....

   d Who has been secretly engaged to Jane
      Fairfax? ....

   e Who is Harriet in love with? ....

After you read

24 What does Emma learn about:

   a speaking unkindly to people who are not her equal?

   b Jane's reasons for taking the job with Mrs Smallridge?

   c Frank's reason for keeping his engagement a secret?

   d her feelings for Mr Knightley?

   e Mrs Weston?

Chapter 9

Before you read

25 Read the title of Chapter 9 and look at the pictures. Who are the people in the picture on page 53? Who do you think marries who? Why?

While you read

26 Circle the correct answer.

a Who first tells Mr Knightley about the marriage between Frank and Jane?
  • Harriet • Emma • Mr Weston

b When Mr Knightley learns that Emma never loved Frank, he is
  • shocked • hopeful • annoyed

c Immediately after Emma tells Mr Knightley that she loves him, they
  • shake hands • go into the house • kiss

d After Mr Knightley leaves, Emma writes to Isabella about
  • Harriet • Mr Knightley • Frank

e Emma tells her father that she and Mr Knightley will live in
  • Hartfield • London • Mr Knightley's house

f Harriet agrees to marry
  • Mr Knightley • Robert Martin • John Knightley

g Mr Knightley explains to Emma why he talked so often to
  • Mr Woodhouse • Frank Churchill • Harriet Smith

h At Randalls, Emma and Frank agree that they have both
  • behaved badly • been in love • disliked Jane

27 Are these sentences true (T) or false (F)?

a Harriet feels foolish when she thinks about her love for Mr Knightley.   .....

b Emma realises that she was right about Robert Martin.   .....

c Mr Elton, the vicar of Highbury Church, marries Harriet and Robert Martin there in September.   .....

d Emma and Mr Knightley want to marry in October but Mr Woodhouse thinks they should wait.   .....

e Mrs Elton is invited but she does not want to go to
such a simple wedding. .....

f Mr Knightley and Emma have a big wedding with
many guests. .....

After you read

28 Who says these words and why?

a 'I seem to have been blind about a lot of things.'

b 'If I loved you less, I might be able to talk about it more.'

c 'It will not work. It is a shocking idea.'

d 'I wanted to get to know her and understand why you liked her
so much.'

e 'I am surprised you did not suspect us.'

29 Discuss the importance of social class in this story. Why does
Harriet marry Robert Martin? What does this teach Emma about
marriage?

30 In Chapter 1, Mr Knightley tells Emma, 'Sensible men do not want
silly wives.' Discuss these questions.

a Does he ever think Emma is silly? Do you think she is? Has
he married a sensible woman in the end? Will they be happy
together and will she stop match-making?

b Why do you think Jane Austen ends the story with three
marriages?

Writing

31 Imagine that you are Harriet Smith and you have just met Emma at
Hartfield. She tells you that Mr Elton thinks you are beautiful and
he wants a painting of you. Write in your diary what you feel about
Emma, Robert Martin, and the possibility of meeting Mr Elton.

32 Imagine you are Mr Knightley. You are angry with Emma for filling
Harriet's head with ideas of high society. Write a letter to Robert
Martin and tell him how unhappy you are about the situation. Give
him some hope and some advice.

33 In what way was Mr Knightley wrong about Harriet, and in what way was Emma wrong about Robert Martin? What gave each of them the wrong idea about these people? Explain how social class affected their opinions.

34 Frank Churchill continually promises to visit his father Mr Weston and his new wife, but he always has an excuse for not visiting. His aunt is jealous and does not want him to go away. Write a conversation between Mr and Mrs Weston after they receive a letter from Frank with another excuse and another promise to visit soon.

35 Write Jane Fairfax's letter to Miss Bates, her aunt, telling her she is coming next week for at least three months. Explain about the Campbells' trip to Ireland and your bad cold.

36 Write a comparison of Mr Knightley and Mr Elton, the vicar. Which is the better man, do you think? Why?

37 Emma learns that match-making can be a dangerous game. Write about the dangers and excitement of match-making for a young people's magazine. Give advice to anyone who wants to be a match-maker.

38 How has the behaviour between unmarried young adults changed since Jane Austen's day? What would she find shocking about today's young people?

39 Who do you think is the most selfish person in this story? Why? Write your opinion and give examples.

40 Choose one of the couples in this story and write about their lives over the next ten years after the story ends.

WORD LIST

adopt (v) to become the legal parent of someone else's child

appear to (v) to seem to

ball (n) a big formal party where people dance

brilliant (adj) very clever

carriage (n) a vehicle pulled by a horse, used for carrying people

delighted (adj) very pleased

delightful (adj) very pleasant or enjoyable

drawing room (n) a large room in a house where people sit, talk and meet visitors

elegant (adj) well-dressed, attractive and moving well

engaged (adj) promised in marriage

fortnight (n) two weeks

gipsy (n) someone who lives and travels around in a home on wheels

impressed (adj) full of admiration

inn (n) a place where you can stop to eat, drink and sometimes sleep, usually in the countryside

match-making (n) trying to find partners for other people to marry

misunderstand (v) to not understand someone or something correctly

obviously (adv) very clearly, in a way that is easy to notice or understand

Papa (n) Father

picnic (n) a meal that you take with you to eat somewhere outdoors

rumour (n) news which that people tell each other without being sure that it is true

sigh (v) to breathe out loudly because you are annoyed or unhappy

strawberry (n) a small sweet red fruit that grows near the ground

suspect (v) to think that someone may be guilty of doing something bad

vicar (n) a person in charge of a church and its religious services in the Church of England

Love Actually
Richard Curtis

In London, Christmas is coming and the people in this story
have love on their minds. Some have found love; some have lost
it. Some accept their loneliness; others live in hope. Even the
new British prime minister's thoughts are not always on his job
– because love, actually, is all around us.

Gone with the Wind – Part One
Margaret Mitchell

Gone with the Wind is a story of love and war and one of the
best-selling books of all time. Part 1 follows the popular but selfish
Scarlett O'Hara, the gentlemanly Ashley Wilkes, and dangerous
but charming Rhett Butler as their world is destroyed in the terrible
American Civil War.

Gone with the Wind – Part Two
Margaret Mitchell

Gone with the Wind is a great romantic story of love and war and
one of the best-selling books of all time. In Part 2, the American
Civil War has destroyed Scarlett O'Hara's comfortable world. Will
she lose her home too? Or can she save it and rebuild her life?

*There are hundreds of Penguin Readers to choose from – world classics,
film adaptations, modern-day crime and adventure, short stories,
biographies, American classics, non-fiction, plays ...*

For a complete list of all Penguin Readers titles, please contact your local
Pearson Longman office or visit our website.

www.penguinreaders.com

The Picture of Dorian Gray
Oscar Wilde

An artist paints a picture of the young and handsome Dorian Gray. When he sees it, Dorian makes a wish that changes his life. As he grows older, his face stays young and handsome. But the picture changes. Why can't Dorian show it to anybody? What is its terrible secret?

Lorna Doone
R. D. Blackmore

In 1673 young John Ridd meets a little girl called Lorna Doone. Seven years later they meet again, and fall in love. But the Doones are a family of robbers and murderers. One of them, Carver, killed John's father and now wants to marry Lorna. Can John save Lorna from her worst fears?

Far from the Madding Crowd
Thomas Hardy

Gabriel Oak is an honest, hard-working young farmer, who falls in love with the beautiful and independent Bathsheba Everdene. After a tragic accident, Gabriel loses his farm. Basheba, on the other hand, becomes rich. Is there any hope for Gabriel?

There are hundreds of Penguin Readers to choose from – world classics, film adaptations, modern-day crime and adventure, short stories, biographies, American classics, non-fiction, plays ...

For a complete list of all Penguin Readers titles, please contact your local Pearson Longman office or visit our website.

www.penguinreaders.com

The Canterville Ghost and Other Stories
Oscar Wilde

The famous Canterville Ghost haunts an old house, but the ghost becomes unhappy when the new owners play tricks on *him*! In the other stories, we meet Lord Arthur Savile, who has to murder someone before he can get married, and we discover the secret life of beautiful Lady Alroy.

The Time Machine
H. G. Wells

The Time Traveller has built a time machine and has gone into the future to the year 802,701. He expects to find a better world with highly intelligent people and great inventions. Instead, he finds that people have become weak, child-like creatures. They dance and sing and wear flowers. They seem happy, but why are they so frightened of the dark? And who or what has taken his time machine? Will the Time Traveller ever be able to return to the present?

Three Adventures of Sherlock Holmes
Sir Arthur Conan Doyle

Sherlock Holmes is a great detective. There are few cases that he cannot solve. In these three stories we meet a young woman who is very frightened of a 'speckled band', a family who think that five orange pips are a sign of death, and banker who believes that his son is a thief. But are things really as they seem?

There are hundreds of Penguin Readers to choose from – world classics, film adaptations, modern-day crime and adventure, short stories, biographies, American classics, non-fiction, plays ...

For a complete list of all Penguin Readers titles, please contact your local Pearson Longman office or visit our website.

www.penguinreaders.com

Longman Dictionaries

Express yourself with confidence!

*Longman has led the way in ELT dictionaries since 1935.
We constantly talk to students and teachers around the
world to find out what they need from a learner's dictionary.*

Why choose a Longman dictionary?

Easy to understand

Longman invented the Defining Vocabulary – 2000 of the most
common words which are used to write the definitions in our
dictionaries. So Longman definitions are always clear and easy
to understand.

Real, natural English

All Longman dictionaries contain natural examples taken from
real-life that help explain the meaning of a word and show you
how to use it in context.

Avoid common mistakes

Longman dictionaries are written specially for learners, and we
make sure that you get all the help you need to avoid common
mistakes. We analyse typical learners' mistakes and include
notes on how to avoid them.

Innovative CD-ROMs

Longman are leaders in dictionary CD-ROM innovation. Did
you know that a dictionary CD-ROM includes features to help
improve your pronunciation, help you practice for exams and
improve your writing skills?

**For details of all Longman dictionaries, and to choose
the one that's right for you, visit our website:**

www.longman.com/dictionaries